THE PRODUCTIVITY PARADOX

UNLOCKING THE SECRETS OF HIGH PERFORMANCE

PRINCE GUPTA

Made with ♥ on the Notion Press Platform
www.notionpress.com

To a bright future, where productivity and procrastination exist in harmony, and every individual has the tools and knowledge to reach their full potential.

This book is dedicated to all those who strive for success, but are held back by the fear of failure and the pull of procrastination. May it serve as a beacon of hope and inspiration, guiding you towards a future filled with abundance, fulfillment, and purpose.

With the power of knowledge and the determination to succeed, you can unlock the secrets of high performance and achieve greatness. The journey may be challenging, but the rewards will be immeasurable.

Here's to a future where every individual is empowered to reach their full potential, where procrastination is no longer a barrier, but a stepping stone to success. Here's to a brighter future for us all.

Contents

Foreword

In today's fast-paced world, productivity is king. The pressure to achieve more, do more, and be more can be overwhelming, and procrastination can quickly become our greatest enemy. Yet, as we all know, the road to success is rarely straightforward.

The relationship between procrastination and productivity is complex and often misunderstood. But what if I told you that procrastination can actually be a valuable tool for unlocking your full potential?

This is the premise of "The Productivity Paradox: Unlocking the Secrets of High Performance". Through a blend of scientific research and practical tips, this book explores the often-maligned relationship between procrastination and productivity, revealing the secrets to unlocking your full potential and achieving success.

As you read this book, you will learn how to harness the power of procrastination, overcome its limitations, and become more productive, efficient, and successful. Whether you're looking to boost your career, improve your personal life, or simply achieve more, "The Productivity Paradox" has the tools and knowledge you need to succeed.

So let's embark on this journey together, towards a brighter future where productivity and procrastination exist in harmony, and every individual has the tools and knowledge to reach their full potential. Here's to a brighter tomorrow.

Foreword

Preface

We've all been there. The deadline is looming, and yet, instead of tackling the task at hand, we find ourselves scrolling through social media, cleaning out the kitchen cabinets, or doing anything but the work that needs to be done. This is procrastination, and for many of us, it's a vicious cycle that can hold us back from reaching our full potential.

But what if I told you that procrastination could actually be a valuable tool for unlocking your full potential? That's the premise of this book, "The Productivity Paradox: Unlocking the Secrets of High Performance".

In this book, we delve into the often-misunderstood relationship between procrastination and productivity, and explore the science behind why we procrastinate and how it affects our performance. With practical tips and strategies for overcoming procrastination and boosting productivity, this book provides a comprehensive guide to achieving success in all areas of life.

Whether you're looking to improve your career, personal life, or simply achieve more, "The Productivity Paradox" has the tools and knowledge you need to succeed. So let's embark on this journey together, towards a future where procrastination is no longer a barrier, but a stepping stone to success.

It's time to unlock the secrets of high performance and achieve greatness. Let's get started.

Acknowledgements

Writing this book would not have been possible without the support and inspiration of many individuals and resources. First and foremost, I would like to express my gratitude to the scientific community for their groundbreaking research and insights into the relationship between procrastination and productivity.

I would also like to thank the team at OpenAI for their work on the advanced AI based tools. The wealth of information, knowledge and vizualization provided by their tools was invaluable in the creation of this book.

I am also deeply grateful to my family and friends, who provided unwavering support and encouragement throughout the writing process.

Finally, I would like to thank you, the reader, for embarking on this journey with me. Your interest and dedication to unlocking the secrets of high performance are what inspired me to write this book, and I hope that it provides you with the tools and knowledge you need to achieve greatness.

Thank you all for your support and encouragement. Here's to a brighter future.

-Author

Prologue

We've all heard the phrase "time is money", and yet, so often, we find ourselves squandering our most valuable resource. Whether it's scrolling through social media, playing video games, or simply putting off a task until tomorrow, procrastination is a constant struggle for many of us.

But what if I told you that procrastination isn't necessarily a bad thing? What if, instead of viewing it as a hindrance to productivity, we embraced it as a tool for unlocking our full potential?

In this book, "The Productivity Paradox: Unlocking the Secrets of High Performance", we delve into the often-misunderstood relationship between procrastination and productivity, and explore the science behind why we procrastinate and how it affects our performance. With practical tips and strategies for overcoming procrastination and boosting productivity, this book provides a comprehensive guide to achieving success in all areas of life.

So join me on this journey, as we discover the secrets to unlocking the full potential of our time and our lives. It's time to turn procrastination into a powerful tool for success.

Know The Author

Meet **Prince Gupta**, a Nepali scholar and bright young mind who is at the forefront of the next generation of tech enthusiasts. Prince is an undergraduate student pursuing a B.Tech in Computer Science Engineering at Jain Deemed to be University in Bangalore, India. He is an ambitious and driven individual who is passionate about technology and its role in shaping our future.

Despite his youth, Prince has already made a name for himself as a visionary thinker, with a deep understanding of the trends and challenges that are shaping our world today. He is always seeking new ways to apply technology to improve our lives and create a better future for all.

Prince's love for technology is matched by his desire to help others achieve their full potential. He has been inspiring and educating others about the possibilities of technology and how they can use it to achieve their goals. He believes that anyone, regardless of their background, can use technology to make a positive impact in their lives and in the world.

With this book, Prince aims to share his insights and knowledge on the important topic of productivity vs procrastination. By drawing on his own experiences and his deep understanding of the latest research, Prince provides readers with practical strategies and tips that they can use to overcome procrastination and achieve their full potential.

So, whether you're a student, a professional, or just someone who wants to get more out of life, Prince's book is the perfect guide to help you unlock the secrets of high performance and reach your goals. So, get ready to embark on a journey of self-discovery and growth with this Nepali scholar, and discover how you can turn procrastination into a tool for success.

CHAPTER I

Introduction

Procrastination is a common enemy that most of us face in our daily lives. It can take many forms, from putting off tasks until tomorrow, avoiding a difficult project, or simply wasting time on unimportant activities. Despite our best efforts, we often find ourselves stuck in a cycle of procrastination, struggling to make progress and reach our goals.

However, the relationship between procrastination and productivity is not as simple as it seems. Research has shown that there are many factors that contribute to procrastination, including our personality traits, environment, and learned behaviors. And while procrastination can be a major barrier to productivity, it can also be a powerful tool for success when used correctly.

This is the paradox of productivity.

In this book, we will delve into the complex relationship between procrastination and productivity and explore the science behind why we procrastinate and how it affects our performance. We will examine the latest research on high performance and the strategies that top performers use to maximize their productivity and minimize their procrastination.

Our goal is to provide you with a comprehensive guide to unlocking the secrets of high performance, and help you turn procrastination into a powerful tool for success.

We will explore the psychological and scientific reasons behind procrastination and provide practical tips and strategies for overcoming procrastination and boosting productivity. We will also examine the science of motivation and provide tips for staying motivated and engaged in your work.

Whether you're a student, entrepreneur, or simply someone looking to achieve more in life, this book will provide you with the tools and knowledge you need to overcome procrastination and take control of your time and your life.

So join us on this journey, as we unlock the secrets of high performance and turn procrastination into a powerful tool for success.

• • •

CHAPTER II

Understanding Procrastination

Definition

Procrastination is a habit that refers to the act of delaying or postponing tasks, activities or decisions that are important or necessary for personal, academic, or professional success. It is a common phenomenon that affects individuals across all age groups, cultures, and backgrounds. The practice of procrastination is often rooted in a lack of motivation, self-doubt, or fear of failure, which can make it difficult for people to start and complete important tasks.

However, the effects of procrastination can be far-reaching and can have a negative impact on an individual's wellbeing, relationships, and career. Chronic procrastination can lead to increased stress, anxiety, and depression, as well as decreased self-esteem, productivity, and success. It can also affect an individual's personal and professional relationships, leading to conflicts and strained connections.

Procrastination is not to be confused with taking a break or taking time to recharge, as these activities are often beneficial and necessary for maintaining good health and well-being. Rather, procrastination refers to the persistent delay of important tasks, even when it is clear that this delay will have negative consequences.

There are many reasons why people procrastinate, including a lack of motivation, disorganization, poor time-management skills, and a tendency to avoid tasks that are challenging or boring. Procrastination can also be linked to underlying psychological and emotional issues, such as anxiety, depression, and low self-esteem.

Despite its negative consequences, procrastination is a habit that can be overcome with the right strategies and techniques. This book will provide readers with a comprehensive understanding of procrastination and explore the reasons behind why we delay tasks. By gaining a deeper insight into the psychology of procrastination, readers will be equipped with the knowledge and tools needed to overcome this habit and boost their productivity.

In conclusion, procrastination is a widespread phenomenon that affects individuals across all age groups and backgrounds. The negative effects of procrastination can be far-reaching, affecting an individual's wellbeing, relationships, and career. However, with the right strategies and techniques, procrastination can be overcome, allowing individuals to achieve greater success and fulfillment in their personal and professional lives.

Prevalence

The prevalence of procrastination is a widespread issue that affects individuals of all ages and backgrounds. It is estimated that around 20% of the population are chronic procrastinators, with this number rising in recent years due to the increasing demands of modern life and the ease of distractions provided by technology.

Procrastination is not just a simple habit or personality trait, but a complex phenomenon that can have significant impacts on our lives. It can lead to increased stress and anxiety, decreased motivation, decreased productivity, and even reduced quality of life.

Research has shown that procrastination is not just limited to students and academics, but also affects professionals, entrepreneurs, and even homemakers. In today's fast-paced world, where everyone is constantly under pressure to achieve more and meet deadlines, procrastination has become a common issue.

The issue of procrastination is further compounded by the fact that it can be a self-perpetuating cycle. When we put off tasks, we often feel stressed and anxious, which in turn leads to further procrastination. This cycle can be difficult to break and can result in long-term negative effects on our mental and physical health.

Procrastination can also lead to decreased productivity and reduced quality of work. When we put off tasks, we often feel stressed and anxious, which in turn reduces our ability to focus and perform at our best. This can result in decreased productivity, missed deadlines, and decreased job satisfaction.

Despite its prevalence and negative effects, procrastination is often not taken seriously and is often seen as a personal weakness or character flaw. However, this view is misguided and it is important to recognize that procrastination is a complex issue that requires a deeper understanding and a multi-faceted approach to overcome.

In conclusion, the prevalence of procrastination is a significant issue that affects individuals from all walks of life. By understanding the underlying causes and effects of procrastination, we can better equip ourselves to overcome it and achieve higher levels of productivity and performance.

Common Reasons

The common reasons for procrastination can vary greatly from person to person, but some of the most frequently cited include:

Fear of failure - Many people delay starting a task because they are afraid they will not perform it well or that the outcome will not be up to their expectations. This fear can be especially pronounced for people who are perfectionists or who are highly critical of their own work.

Perfectionism - Some individuals may be overly focused on getting everything just right, which can cause them to delay starting a task until they have all the necessary information, resources or tools to do so. This can be especially problematic when the task at hand is complex or challenging.

Lack of motivation - When people are not excited about a task or do not see its relevance, they may be less likely to start working on it. This can be especially true for tasks that are seen as mundane, tedious or uninteresting.

Overwhelm - Sometimes people are so intimidated by the size of a task that they put it off until they feel more prepared to tackle it. This can also be the case when there are many tasks that need to be done and people do not know where to start.

Distractions - With the advent of technology and the Internet, people are constantly bombarded by notifications, messages and calls, making it difficult for them to stay focused on their work. As a result, some individuals may choose to procrastinate and put off their work until later.

Disorganization - People who struggle with disorganization or poor time-management skills may find it difficult to prioritize their tasks and get started on the work that is most important.

Poor self-discipline - People who struggle with self-discipline may find it difficult to resist distractions and to get started on a task. This can be especially problematic when there are other activities or habits that are more enjoyable or satisfying.

Low energy levels - Sometimes people may be too tired or lacking energy to start a task, so they put it off until they have more energy or feel more refreshed.

Resistance to change - Some individuals may be resistant to change or to doing things differently than they have in the past. This can lead to procrastination when the task at hand requires them to try new approaches or methods.

Depression and anxiety - Individuals who are struggling with depression or anxiety may find it difficult to focus on their work and to get started on tasks, leading to procrastination.

These are just some of the common reasons why people procrastinate. By understanding the underlying causes of procrastination, individuals can work to overcome it and increase their productivity.

Psychological Factors

Procrastination is a complex phenomenon that can be influenced by a range of psychological factors. These factors can vary from person to person and can be influenced by an individual's personality, beliefs, values, and past experiences. Understanding the psychological factors that contribute to procrastination can be an important step towards overcoming it.

Personality Traits

One of the key psychological factors that can contribute to procrastination is an individual's personality traits. People with certain personality traits, such as impulsiveness, low self-esteem, and high anxiety, may be more prone to procrastination. For example, people who are highly impulsive may struggle to resist the urge to delay tasks in favor of more immediate pleasures. On the other hand, people with low self-esteem may avoid tasks that they feel are beyond their abilities, leading to procrastination.

Beliefs and Values

Another key factor that can contribute to procrastination is an individual's beliefs and values. For example, some people may have a belief that they work best under pressure and therefore procrastinate in order to meet a tight deadline. Other people may prioritize leisure time and put off tasks that they view as unenjoyable or less important. These beliefs and values can lead to procrastination as people prioritize other things over the tasks they need to complete.

Past Experiences

Past experiences can also play a role in procrastination. For example, people who have experienced failure or setbacks in the past may be more likely to avoid tasks that they associate with negative outcomes. They may also be more likely to put off tasks that are challenging or outside of their comfort zones, for fear of experiencing similar failures in the future.

Emotional Regulation

Another key psychological factor that can contribute to procrastination is emotional regulation. People who struggle with regulating their emotions may find it difficult to focus on tasks and may put off work in order to avoid feelings of stress, anxiety, or frustration. They may also be more likely to seek out distractions or engage in activities that provide temporary relief from these negative emotions.

In conclusion, understanding the psychological factors that contribute to procrastination can be an important step towards overcoming it. By recognizing the underlying causes of procrastination, individuals can better equip themselves to address these issues and improve their productivity. Whether it's by developing better coping mechanisms, changing beliefs and values, or seeking support from friends and family, taking steps to address the psychological factors behind procrastination can help people to lead more productive and fulfilling lives

The Negative Impact

The negative impact of procrastination on our lives and productivity cannot be overstated. Procrastination has far-reaching consequences that can affect not only our work and careers but also our mental and physical health.

One of the most immediate effects of procrastination is stress. When we put off tasks until the last minute, we are often rushing to complete them, which can lead to increased stress levels and anxiety. This stress can interfere with our ability to focus and be productive, making it even more difficult to get things done.

Procrastination can also have a damaging impact on our confidence and self-esteem. When we constantly put off tasks and fail to meet deadlines, we may start to feel as though we are not good enough or capable of succeeding. This can lead to a vicious cycle of self-doubt, procrastination, and further stress.

Procrastination can also harm our relationships and social life. When we put off tasks, we may not be able to spend time with friends and family, or participate in hobbies and activities that we enjoy. This can lead to feelings of isolation and loneliness, which can further impact our mental and emotional wellbeing.

Finally, procrastination can also have serious financial consequences. When we miss deadlines and fail to complete tasks, we may lose out on opportunities for promotions, bonuses, or other financial rewards. Additionally, when we put off tasks for too long, we may end up paying more for goods or services, or may even incur penalties or fees.

In conclusion, procrastination is a habit that can have far-reaching and damaging effects on our lives. By recognizing the negative impact of procrastination, we can take steps to overcome it and lead a more productive and fulfilling life.

Overcoming Procrastination

Procrastination can be a formidable foe, but with the right tools and strategies, it is possible to overcome. The key to success is to identify the root causes of your procrastination and to develop strategies to combat them.

One common strategy is to break tasks down into smaller, manageable parts. This helps to reduce the anxiety and overwhelm associated with large tasks and makes it easier to get started. Another strategy is to use a timer. This helps to structure your workday and gives you a sense of accomplishment as you complete each task.

Goal setting is another important tool in overcoming procrastination. Set realistic, achievable goals that are aligned with your values and interests. Focus on making progress, rather than perfection, and remember that small steps forward are better than none at all.

Mindfulness is another key tool in overcoming procrastination. By paying attention to the present moment, you can cultivate a sense of calm and reduce stress and anxiety. Mindfulness also helps you to identify when you are procrastinating, so you can take steps to overcome it.

Accountability is another important tool in overcoming procrastination. Work with a coach or mentor who can provide you with support, encouragement, and accountability. Join a support group or online community where you can share your progress and get feedback and support.

Finally, it is important to cultivate a growth mindset. This means embracing challenges as opportunities for growth and learning, rather than as obstacles or failures. With a growth mindset, you can approach each task with a positive attitude, knowing that you will learn and grow from the experience.

In conclusion, overcoming procrastination is a journey that requires patience, persistence, and a willingness to try new strategies and approaches. Remember that success is not a destination, but a journey, and that each step forward is a step in the right direction. With the right tools and strategies, you can overcome procrastination and achieve the high performance you desire.

The Need

The need to overcome procrastination and boost productivity is paramount in today's fast-paced world. The constant barrage of distractions and competing priorities can make it difficult to stay focused and on task. The allure of procrastination can be strong, but it ultimately leads to decreased productivity, decreased quality of work, and decreased overall satisfaction with life.

Procrastination can lead to increased stress and anxiety as deadlines loom and tasks pile up. It can also cause feelings of guilt and shame as we fail to meet our own expectations and let others down. These negative emotions can have a significant impact on our mental health and overall well-being.

Furthermore, procrastination can lead to missed opportunities and lost revenue. When we put off important tasks, we may miss deadlines, lose out on promotions or job opportunities, or even miss out on valuable business deals.

In order to succeed in today's fast-paced world, it is crucial to develop the skills and strategies necessary to overcome procrastination and boost productivity. This requires a deep understanding of the root causes of procrastination and a commitment to developing new habits and strategies for success. By recognizing the need to overcome procrastination and taking proactive steps to do so, we can achieve our goals and achieve a sense of fulfillment and satisfaction in life.

CHAPTER III

The Productivity Paradox

Understanding the Concept

The concept of productivity paradox refers to the phenomenon in which increased productivity does not always lead to improved results or outcomes. It suggests that the more time and effort we put into our work, the better our results should be, but this is not always the case.

To understand the productivity paradox, it is important to first understand the definition of productivity. Productivity refers to the efficiency of converting inputs into outputs. In the context of work, this means turning the time and effort invested into results or outputs that are of value to us and to others.

The paradox arises when we put in more time and effort, but do not see the expected improvement in outcomes. For example, if you spend more time working on a project, you would expect the quality and quantity of your output to increase. However, if the increase in time and effort does not result in an improvement in the quality and quantity of your output, then you are experiencing the productivity paradox.

There are several factors that contribute to the productivity paradox, including lack of focus, poor time management, and lack of motivation. When we are not focused, we waste time and effort on distractions, and this can reduce our overall productivity. Poor time management can lead to procrastination, as we put off tasks that are important but not urgent, and this can also reduce our productivity. Finally, lack of motivation can lead to reduced engagement and effort, which can also negatively impact our productivity.

To overcome the productivity paradox, it is important to understand the underlying causes and to put in place strategies to address them. This might include improving our focus, practicing better time management, and finding ways to increase our motivation. By doing so, we can increase our productivity and achieve better results.

In conclusion, the productivity paradox is a phenomenon that affects many people and can have negative impacts on our work and personal lives. However, by understanding the concept and putting in place strategies to overcome it, we can improve our productivity and achieve better outcomes.

The Roots

The roots of the productivity paradox lie in the complex and intertwined relationship between our behavior, motivation, and the environment. At its core, the paradox is a result of the misalignment between our intentions and actions. We often set out with the goal of being productive, but somehow, we end up procrastinating and fall short of our expectations.

One of the primary reasons behind the productivity paradox is the nature of our brains. The human brain is designed to be efficient and conserve energy. It tends to avoid tasks that require significant effort and will often choose the path of least resistance. This is why we are often tempted to procrastinate and put off important tasks for later.

Another key factor contributing to the productivity paradox is our environment. Our surroundings, whether it be our home, office, or school, can have a profound impact on our behavior and motivation. For example, if our work environment is cluttered and disorganized, it can cause distractions and impede our ability to focus on tasks. Similarly, if we don't have a clear structure or routine in place, we may find it difficult to manage our time effectively and prioritize our tasks.

The impact of technology on our lives is also a contributing factor to the productivity paradox. With so many distractions and instant gratification options available at our fingertips, it's easy to become addicted to our devices and lose track of time. This constant distraction can lead to decreased focus, reduced motivation, and ultimately, decreased productivity.

Finally, our personal beliefs and attitudes play a role in the productivity paradox. If we have a fixed mindset and believe that our abilities are limited, we may be less likely to challenge ourselves and strive for growth. On the other hand, if we have a growth mindset and believe that we can always improve and develop new skills, we are more likely to push ourselves and strive for higher levels of productivity.

In conclusion, the productivity paradox is a complex and multifaceted issue that stems from a variety of factors, including our brain, environment, technology, and personal beliefs and attitudes. By gaining a deeper understanding of these roots, we can better equip ourselves to overcome the paradox and achieve our productivity goals.

The Balancing Act

Productivity is often viewed as the key to success in today's fast-paced and demanding world. However, it can be easy to fall into the trap of trying to do too much, too fast, and too soon. The result is often burnout, decreased motivation, and decreased overall productivity. This is where the importance of finding the right balance between productivity and relaxation comes into play. In order to maintain high performance, it's essential to find a way to balance the demands of work and the need for rest and rejuvenation.

The first step in finding the right balance is to understand the difference between productive and unproductive time. Productive time is time spent working on tasks that are important and have clear goals, while unproductive time is time spent on activities that do not contribute to your goals. This can include time spent watching TV, browsing the internet, or engaging in other leisure activities. It's important to recognize the value of both productive and unproductive time, as they both play a role in our overall well-being.

Another important factor in finding the right balance between productivity and relaxation is setting realistic goals. It's important to set achievable goals for each day, week, and month, and to prioritize these goals based on their importance. This will help you stay focused and motivated, and will also ensure that you are not overwhelming yourself with too many tasks. It's also important to take breaks regularly and to engage in activities that help you relax and recharge, such as meditation, yoga, or spending time with friends and family.

One of the most important elements of finding the right balance between productivity and relaxation is learning to manage your time effectively. This includes developing a daily routine, using time-management tools and techniques, and being proactive in addressing time-wasters. For example, setting aside specific times for email and social media can help you avoid getting distracted from your work. Additionally, it's important to learn how to say "no" to non-essential tasks and activities, so that you can focus your time and energy on the things that matter most.

Finally, it's important to cultivate a growth mindset and to be open to new experiences and challenges. By embracing change and being open to new ideas and perspectives, you can continue to grow and evolve, and you can also find new ways to balance productivity and relaxation. By focusing on your personal growth and development, you can not only maintain high performance, but also lead a fulfilling and satisfying life.

In conclusion, finding the right balance between productivity and relaxation is crucial for high performance. By understanding the concept of the productivity paradox, setting realistic goals, managing your time effectively, and embracing change, you can unlock the secrets of high performance and achieve your full potential.

The Impact of Technology

Technology has revolutionized the way we live and work, providing us with new tools and resources to boost our productivity. But it has also led to the creation of the productivity paradox, where people are able to work longer hours and produce more work than ever before, but also feel more overwhelmed and stressed. The impact of technology on productivity is complex and multi-faceted, with both positive and negative effects.

On the positive side, technology has allowed us to be more connected and efficient. We can now communicate with colleagues and clients from anywhere in the world, and access information and resources at the click of a button. This has made it easier for people to work remotely, and for businesses to expand globally.

Technology has also enabled us to automate many tasks, freeing up time for more creative and strategic work. For example, we can use tools like project management software to organize tasks and deadlines, or time tracking software to monitor our productivity. This can help us to work more efficiently and effectively, allowing us to get more done in less time.

However, technology can also have negative effects on our productivity. For example, the constant barrage of notifications and distractions from our phones, laptops and other devices can make it difficult to focus and complete tasks. We may also feel the need to constantly check our devices, even when we should be relaxing and recharging. This can lead to burnout, decreased motivation and decreased productivity.

Moreover, technology has created new forms of procrastination, such as scrolling through social media, watching videos, or playing games. These activities may seem like harmless distractions, but they can quickly consume our time and reduce our productivity.

In conclusion, technology has had a profound impact on our productivity, both positive and negative. To make the most of the benefits of technology, we need to strike a balance between utilizing its resources and avoiding its distractions. This requires discipline, focus and the ability to prioritize our time and tasks effectively. By understanding the impact of technology on productivity, we can make informed choices that will help us to work smarter, not harder, and achieve a healthy work-life balance.

The Modern Workplace

The modern workplace has been undergoing a significant transformation in the last few decades. With advancements in technology and the rise of the gig economy, the way we work and the expectations placed upon us have changed dramatically. In this fast-paced, always-on world, it's more important than ever to find a healthy balance between productivity and relaxation. Unfortunately, this is easier said than done. The modern workplace is a breeding ground for the productivity paradox, a phenomenon where the more we work, the less productive we become.

One of the main drivers of this paradox is the constant distraction and barrage of information we face in the digital age. The Internet has made it easier than ever to access information, but it has also made it harder to focus and complete tasks. We are constantly bombarded by emails, messages, and notifications, which can pull us away from our work and make it more difficult to be productive. Furthermore, with the rise of remote work, it's becoming increasingly difficult to separate work from our personal life. This can lead to feelings of burnout and decreased productivity.

Another factor contributing to the productivity paradox is the increasing workloads and demands placed upon us in the modern workplace. In order to stay competitive, many employees are taking on more responsibilities and working longer hours. However, this often leads to a decrease in productivity, as we become exhausted and overburdened. Furthermore, the pressure to always be productive can also lead to a lack of creativity and innovation. This is because when we are constantly working, we do not have the time or energy to reflect and come up with new ideas.

To overcome the productivity paradox, it is important to understand the root causes and find a healthy balance between work and relaxation. This requires taking control of our time and limiting distractions, as well as finding ways to reduce stress and increase focus. Furthermore, companies must also play a role in addressing the productivity paradox. This can be done by providing employees with the tools and support they need to be productive, as well as fostering a workplace culture that values work-life balance.

In conclusion, the productivity paradox is a real and pressing issue in the modern workplace. To overcome it, we must understand the root causes and find a balance between productivity and relaxation. By doing so, we can not only boost our personal productivity, but also drive innovation and growth in our organizations.

Time Management

Time management is an essential aspect of productivity. It is the process of organizing and planning how you spend your time in order to achieve specific goals and objectives. In today's fast-paced world, time management has become even more critical as people struggle to balance their personal and professional lives. The concept of the productivity paradox is closely linked to time management, as it is believed that improving time management skills can help people become more productive.

At its core, time management is about making choices about what is important to you and what you want to achieve. When people are faced with multiple demands on their time, it can be challenging to prioritize and make effective use of their time. Many people procrastinate or waste time on unimportant tasks, which can impact their productivity and make it difficult to achieve their goals.

One of the key aspects of time management is setting priorities. When you have a clear understanding of what is most important to you, it becomes easier to allocate your time and energy in a way that supports your goals. It is essential to be realistic about what you can and cannot achieve in a given time frame. Setting goals that are too ambitious can lead to frustration and disappointment, so it is important to take small, achievable steps towards your goals.

Another important aspect of time management is learning to say no. People often find themselves overcommitted and struggling to keep up with their responsibilities. This can lead to feelings of stress and burnout. Learning to say no to non-essential tasks and commitments can help you focus your time and energy on what is truly important.

Time management also involves making effective use of technology. There are many tools and apps available that can help you stay organized and manage your time. For example, you can use a task manager app to create to-do lists, set reminders, and track your progress towards your goals. These tools can be extremely helpful in improving your productivity, but it is important to use them judiciously and not let technology take over your life.

The productivity paradox is a complex issue that is closely linked to time management. Improving your time management skills and finding the right balance between productivity and relaxation can help you overcome the paradox and become more productive. By taking a holistic approach to time management and focusing on what is truly important, you can achieve your goals and find a sense of fulfillment in your work.

• • •

CHAPTER IV

The Science of High Performance

The science of high performance is a study of the principles and practices that enable individuals and organizations to achieve exceptional levels of productivity, success, and fulfillment. It encompasses a range of disciplines including psychology, neuroscience, productivity, and wellness, and seeks to understand the factors that influence our ability to perform at our best. From optimizing our time management and developing positive habits to fostering positive relationships and building resilience, the science of high performance provides a comprehensive framework for achieving our full potential. Whether you're an entrepreneur, student, or anyone looking to achieve more in life, understanding the science of high performance is essential to unlocking your full potential.

The Importance of Sleep and Rest

In the fast-paced world of today, sleep and rest are often overlooked and considered as luxurious waste of time. However, the truth is far from this notion. Sleep and rest are vital components of a healthy lifestyle and play a crucial role in boosting one's performance.

Adequate sleep is crucial for physical and mental recovery. During sleep, the body works to repair and rejuvenate cells and tissues, allowing us to perform at our best the next day. Studies have shown that poor sleep habits can lead to decreased cognitive performance, slower reaction times, and reduced energy levels. Furthermore, it can also lead to long-term health problems such as obesity, cardiovascular diseases, and depression.

In addition to sleep, rest is also a crucial part of high performance. The body and mind need time to unwind and recharge, and taking regular breaks from work can help boost creativity and productivity. Relaxation techniques such as deep breathing, meditation, and yoga can help reduce stress and improve overall well-being.

In conclusion, the science of high performance highlights the importance of sleep and rest as critical components of a healthy lifestyle. Neglecting sleep and rest can lead to decreased performance and long-term health problems, making it imperative for individuals to prioritize and prioritize their sleep and relaxation needs. By doing so, individuals can achieve higher levels of performance, both in their personal and professional lives.

The Power of Positive Thinking

The power of positive thinking is a concept that has been around for centuries, but its importance in our lives cannot be overstated. Positive thinking is not just a fleeting emotion or an occasional mood, but a deliberate and conscious choice that we make every day. It involves reframing negative thoughts into positive ones, focusing on what is good in our lives, and cultivating an optimistic outlook on the future. This approach can have a profound impact on our mental and physical health, relationships, and overall quality of life.

Research has shown that people who practice positive thinking have lower levels of stress, anxiety, and depression. They also have stronger immune systems and are more likely to lead happy, fulfilling lives. Positive thinking helps us to better cope with difficult situations, such as losing a job, a loved one, or facing health problems. It gives us the strength and resilience to push through tough times and come out on the other side with a sense of gratitude and hope.

Moreover, positive thinking has a spillover effect on those around us. It is contagious, and when we radiate positivity, we inspire others to do the same. This can lead to a virtuous cycle, where the positive energy in our environment creates a supportive and uplifting environment. Our positive thoughts and actions have the power to create a ripple effect, touching the lives of those around us and improving the world as a whole.

In conclusion, the power of positive thinking is a transformative force that can greatly enhance our lives. By embracing this approach, we can create a brighter future for ourselves and those around us. So, let us make a conscious effort to cultivate a positive outlook, and watch as our lives become enriched and filled with joy, hope, and peace.

Maximizing Physical Performance

Maximizing Physical Performance is an important aspect of high performance. Physical performance is the measure of an individual's ability to perform physical activities efficiently and effectively. Whether it's running, jumping, lifting weights, or playing a sport, physical performance has a direct impact on our ability to reach our goals and perform at our best.

There are a variety of factors that contribute to physical performance, including strength, speed, agility, endurance, and flexibility. A strong focus on physical performance can help individuals build resilience and the ability to perform under stress, increase energy levels, and improve overall health and well-being.

One of the key aspects of maximizing physical performance is developing a consistent exercise routine. Exercise not only helps to increase muscle strength and endurance, but it also has numerous mental health benefits, such as reducing anxiety and stress, and improving overall mood. Additionally, consuming a balanced diet that is rich in nutrients and vitamins is crucial for fueling the body and supporting physical performance.

Staying hydrated is another important factor to consider when maximizing physical performance. Water plays a vital role in the body's ability to function effectively, as it helps to regulate body temperature, transport nutrients, and flush out waste.

Finally, incorporating proper recovery and rest into a physical performance routine is essential for maximizing performance and avoiding injury. This can include activities such as stretching, foam rolling, or taking time for rest and relaxation.

By prioritizing physical performance, individuals can take their performance to the next level and achieve their goals with ease. Whether the goal is to run a faster mile, improve athletic performance, or simply feel more energetic and healthy, focusing on physical performance is a powerful tool for unlocking our full potential.

Eating for Success

Eating for success is a crucial component of the science of high performance. Our bodies require the proper nutrients and fuel to perform at peak levels and sustain high levels of productivity. Consuming a balanced and nutritious diet has been proven to enhance mental clarity, improve mood and overall health, boost energy levels, and sharpen focus.

However, with busy schedules and fast-paced lifestyles, many individuals find it challenging to eat healthily and make nutritious food choices. Convenient junk food and processed snacks are often the go-to options, leading to unhealthy habits and a decline in overall physical performance.

On the other hand, incorporating a variety of nutrient-dense foods in your diet can provide you with the energy, vitamins, and minerals you need to perform at your best. Fruits and vegetables, whole grains, lean proteins, and healthy fats are essential components of a healthy and balanced diet that can help support high performance.

Additionally, it's important to consider portion control and limit the consumption of sugary drinks and processed foods. Staying hydrated is also crucial, as it can improve cognitive function, physical performance, and overall well-being.

In conclusion, eating for success is a critical aspect of the science of high performance. By making smart food choices and nourishing our bodies with the right nutrients, we can optimize our performance, increase productivity, and achieve success.

The Benefits of Mindfulness and Meditation

The benefits of mindfulness and meditation are widely recognized and have been supported by numerous scientific studies. Mindfulness, the act of being present in the moment, and meditation, a practice that involves focusing on the present moment and quieting the mind, have been shown to have a positive impact on physical, mental, and emotional well-being.

Studies have found that mindfulness and meditation can help reduce stress, lower blood pressure, improve sleep, and boost the immune system. Additionally, mindfulness and meditation can help improve focus, increase self-awareness, and foster a sense of inner peace.

One of the primary benefits of mindfulness and meditation is the ability to manage stress and anxiety. When we are stressed or anxious, our minds can become cluttered and chaotic, which can make it difficult to focus and be productive. Mindfulness and meditation can help calm the mind, allowing us to better handle difficult situations and think more clearly.

Meditation has also been shown to improve focus and concentration. By quieting the mind, we are able to eliminate distractions and better focus on the task at hand. This can result in increased productivity and improved performance in work and daily life.

Mindfulness and meditation can also improve our emotional well-being. By paying attention to our thoughts and feelings, we can gain a greater understanding of our own emotions and learn how to better manage them. This can lead to increased self-awareness and a greater sense of inner peace.

In conclusion, the benefits of mindfulness and meditation are numerous and wide-ranging. Whether you're looking to reduce stress and anxiety, improve focus and productivity, or simply improve your overall well-being, incorporating mindfulness and meditation into your daily routine is a step in the right direction. So, take the time to focus on the present moment, quiet your mind, and experience the many benefits of mindfulness and meditation for yourself.

• • •

CHAPTER V

Overcoming Procrastination

Understanding the Causes and Triggers

Procrastination is a common issue faced by people of all ages and walks of life. Despite the widespread nature of this problem, it is often misunderstood and dismissed as a simple lack of motivation or discipline. However, the root causes of procrastination are much more complex and can stem from a variety of psychological, emotional, and environmental factors. Understanding these triggers is crucial in overcoming procrastination and achieving success in both personal and professional aspects of life.

One of the most common causes of procrastination is anxiety and fear. Many people delay starting a task because they are afraid of failing or of not being able to complete it to their satisfaction. This fear can be so strong that it actually becomes easier to avoid the task altogether than to face the anxiety that comes with it. This can lead to a vicious cycle of procrastination, which can be difficult to break.

Another major cause of procrastination is lack of motivation. Many people simply do not feel motivated to complete a task, often because it is not meaningful or interesting to them. This lack of motivation can be due to a variety of reasons, including boredom, lack of clear goals, or feelings of inadequacy.

Poor time management and poor organization skills can also lead to procrastination. If a person feels overwhelmed with tasks and lacks the tools to effectively manage their time, they may find it easier to delay or avoid tasks altogether.

Finally, distractions and procrastination can be triggered by external factors, such as technology, social media, or other forms of entertainment. These distractions can be incredibly tempting, especially when a person is feeling overwhelmed or stressed.

In conclusion, there is no single cause of procrastination, and overcoming this issue requires an understanding of the unique triggers and factors that contribute to it in each individual case.

Developing Self-Awareness and Setting Clear Goals

Developing self-awareness and setting clear goals are two key elements in overcoming procrastination. Procrastination can be a complex issue, with multiple causes and triggers that vary from person to person. Understanding these causes and triggers is the first step in effectively addressing and overcoming procrastination.

Self-awareness is the foundation of personal growth and development. It involves taking an honest look at yourself and your habits, including those that contribute to procrastination. By gaining a deeper understanding of your thoughts, feelings, and behaviors, you can identify the root causes of your procrastination and develop strategies to address them.

Setting clear goals is also essential to overcoming procrastination. Without clear goals, it can be difficult to determine what you should be focusing on and when. Goals provide a roadmap for your life, helping you prioritize your time and energy in a way that aligns with your values and aspirations. They also give you a sense of purpose and motivation, helping you stay focused and on track.

When developing self-awareness and setting clear goals, it's important to be specific and concrete. Start by defining what you want to achieve, breaking down large goals into smaller, manageable tasks. Then, establish a timeline for each task, including deadlines for completion. This structure will help you stay accountable and focused on what you need to do to achieve your goals.

In addition to developing self-awareness and setting clear goals, it's also important to cultivate a growth mindset. This means embracing challenges and viewing setbacks as opportunities to learn and grow, rather than as reasons to give up. By developing a growth mindset, you can overcome the fear and anxiety that often contribute to procrastination, allowing you to focus on your goals and move forward with confidence.

Ultimately, overcoming procrastination is about taking control of your life and your time. By developing self-awareness, setting clear goals, and cultivating a growth mindset, you can achieve the success and fulfillment you desire.

Implementing Effective Time Management Strategies

Time management is one of the key components of overcoming procrastination and increasing productivity. It is essential to understand that time management is not just about working harder or longer, but about working smarter and making the most of the time you have. There are many popular strategies that can help individuals implement effective time management, but three of the most effective are prioritizing, delegating, and scheduling.

Prioritizing is a crucial aspect of time management. It involves identifying the most important tasks and focusing on completing them first, while setting aside less important tasks for later. By prioritizing tasks, individuals can ensure that they are using their time in the most productive way possible, and that they are making the greatest impact with their efforts.

Delegating is another important aspect of time management. This involves transferring tasks to others who are better equipped to handle them, freeing up valuable time that can be spent on more important tasks. Delegating is particularly important for those who struggle with procrastination, as it helps to reduce the number of tasks that need to be done, reducing the chance of becoming overwhelmed.

Finally, scheduling is a powerful tool for managing time. This involves setting aside specific blocks of time for specific tasks, and following this schedule as closely as possible. By doing so, individuals can ensure that they are dedicating enough time to each task, and that they are not getting sidetracked by other distractions. Additionally, by using a schedule, individuals can better plan for the future, ensuring that they are prepared for any upcoming deadlines or appointments.

In conclusion, by implementing effective time management strategies, individuals can overcome procrastination and increase their productivity. By prioritizing, delegating, and scheduling, individuals can take control of their time and use it to achieve their goals and reach their full potential. These strategies are simple to implement, but can have a profound impact on productivity and success.

Adopting Positive Thinking and a Growth Mindset

Adopting Positive Thinking and a Growth Mindset is a critical aspect of overcoming procrastination. This is because having a positive mindset helps to increase motivation and drive, and a growth mindset helps to build resilience and perseverance in the face of obstacles. In this chapter, we will delve into the importance of positive thinking and a growth mindset in overcoming procrastination and how to cultivate these traits in your life.

First and foremost, it's important to understand what positive thinking and a growth mindset entail. Positive thinking involves focusing on the good things in life and looking for the best in every situation. It involves finding joy in life and being optimistic, even when things are not going as planned. On the other hand, a growth mindset is the belief that one's abilities and talents can be developed through hard work and dedication. It's the belief that challenges and failures are not setbacks, but opportunities for growth and learning.

Having a positive mindset can be especially beneficial when it comes to overcoming procrastination. Positive thinking helps to increase motivation and drive, making it easier to tackle tasks and stick with them. It also helps to reduce stress and anxiety, which can be significant contributors to procrastination. When you're feeling good, it's much easier to get started on tasks and stick with them, which is why positive thinking is so important.

Similarly, a growth mindset is also crucial in overcoming procrastination. People with a growth mindset are more likely to be persistent in the face of obstacles and setbacks, which is essential when overcoming procrastination. They are less likely to give up when things get tough, and instead, they will continue to push forward, knowing that they have the potential to grow and improve. This persistence is critical in overcoming procrastination, as it helps you to stay focused and on track, even when things are not going as planned.

So how do you cultivate positive thinking and a growth mindset? Here are a few tips to get you started:

Practice gratitude. This involves focusing on the things in your life that you're grateful for and taking time to appreciate them. When you're feeling grateful, it's much easier to find joy in life, even when things are not going as planned.

Surround yourself with positive people. People who are positive and supportive can help to uplift your mood and encourage you when you're feeling down. Having positive relationships in your life is critical in building a positive outlook.

Reframe negative thoughts. When negative thoughts enter your mind, try to reframe them into a more positive perspective. This can help to reduce stress and anxiety, and increase motivation and drive.

Engage in self-reflection. Take time to reflect on your thoughts and beliefs about yourself and your abilities. Are there any limiting beliefs that you need to change? Are there any negative thought patterns that you need to challenge?

Focus on progress, not perfection. A growth mindset is all about focusing on progress and growth, rather than perfection. When you focus on your progress, it's much easier to build resilience and perseverance in the face of obstacles and setbacks.

In conclusion, adopting positive thinking and a growth mindset is critical in overcoming procrastination. Positive thinking helps to increase motivation and drive, while a growth mindset helps to build resilience and perseverance. By focusing on gratitude, surrounding yourself with positive people, reframing negative thoughts, engaging in self-reflection, and focusing on progress, you can cultivate these traits in your life and overcome procrastination for good.

Building Self-Discipline and Avoiding Distractions.

Building self-discipline and avoiding distractions are two crucial components in overcoming procrastination and achieving high productivity. By developing self-discipline and avoiding distractions, individuals can increase their focus and stay on track towards their goals.

Self-discipline is the ability to control one's impulses, emotions, and actions in order to meet long-term goals. It is the foundation of any productive behavior and a key factor in overcoming procrastination. When individuals are disciplined, they are better equipped to manage their time and prioritize their tasks effectively.

Distractions, on the other hand, are a major obstacle to productivity. They can come in many forms, such as social media, emails, phone calls, and other forms of technology. They not only divert our attention away from the task at hand but also disrupt our focus and concentration. To avoid distractions, it is important to identify what causes them and eliminate or minimize their impact.

One effective strategy for building self-discipline and avoiding distractions is to develop a routine. This involves creating a set schedule for completing tasks and sticking to it. For example, one could allocate specific times for working, studying, or relaxing. This helps individuals prioritize their time and focus on the most important tasks.

Another approach is to use time management techniques, such as the Pomodoro Technique. This involves breaking down work into 25-minute intervals, with 5-minute breaks in between. This allows individuals to focus for a short amount of time, which can help increase their productivity and motivation.

A third approach is to limit exposure to distractions by setting boundaries and turning off notifications on devices. This helps individuals stay focused and reduces the impact of distractions on their productivity.

In conclusion, building self-discipline and avoiding distractions are important steps in overcoming procrastination and increasing productivity. By developing a routine, using time management techniques, and limiting exposure to distractions, individuals can create a more productive and focused environment, allowing them to achieve their goals and reach new levels of success.

• • •

CHAPTER VI

Staying Motivated

Staying motivated is a crucial aspect of overcoming procrastination and achieving high performance. Without motivation, it is easy to fall back into old habits and let procrastination take control. It is important to understand that motivation is not a constant state, but rather it fluctuates and can be influenced by external and internal factors. In order to stay motivated, it is necessary to regularly assess one's level of motivation and take proactive steps to maintain and boost it.

Setting realistic and attainable goals - Having specific and well-defined goals can provide direction and purpose to one's efforts. When goals are achievable, it provides a sense of accomplishment and drives motivation.

Tracking progress - Keeping track of progress towards goals can help to stay motivated. By regularly reviewing progress, individuals can acknowledge their accomplishments and adjust their approach as needed to continue making progress.

Surrounding yourself with supportive people - Having a strong support system can make a big difference in maintaining motivation. Surrounding oneself with individuals who believe in one's goals and provide encouragement can help to stay motivated and on track.

Celebrating successes - Recognizing and celebrating small victories along the way can help to maintain motivation. Celebrating successes, no matter how small, can provide a sense of accomplishment and boost morale.

Embracing challenges and setbacks - Accepting that setbacks and challenges are a natural part of the process can help to maintain motivation. Rather than getting discouraged by challenges, individuals should embrace them as opportunities for growth and learning.

In conclusion, staying motivated is a key factor in overcoming procrastination and achieving high performance. By setting realistic goals, tracking progress, surrounding oneself with supportive people, celebrating successes, and embracing challenges, individuals can maintain and boost their motivation to achieve their desired outcomes.

CHAPTER VII

Balancing Work and Life

Balancing work and life is one of the biggest challenges faced by people in today's fast-paced world. With the rise of technology and the ability to work from anywhere, it's becoming increasingly difficult to separate our professional lives from our personal lives. The result is that many people are working longer hours, sacrificing their health, relationships and personal lives in pursuit of success.

However, it is important to recognize that this imbalance can have a significant negative impact on our overall well-being and productivity. Studies have shown that people who are unable to balance work and life effectively tend to experience increased levels of stress, burnout, and even physical health problems. On the other hand, those who are able to strike a balance between their professional and personal lives tend to be happier, more fulfilled and more productive in both areas.

To achieve a healthy balance between work and life, it's important to first understand what is truly important to you and what you value most. This can help you make decisions about how you want to allocate your time and energy, and ensure that you are living a life that aligns with your values and priorities.

Next, it's important to set clear boundaries between work and life. This can include things like setting specific times for work and for leisure activities, establishing work-free zones in your home, and avoiding work-related activities during personal time.

Another key aspect of balancing work and life is practicing self-care. This means taking the time to engage in activities that recharge and rejuvenate you, such as exercise, meditation, and spending time with friends and family. Regularly taking breaks and engaging in self-care activities can help reduce stress and improve your overall well-being.

In addition, being mindful of the way you use technology can also help you balance work and life. This means being intentional about when and how you use your devices, and avoiding the temptation to constantly check emails, social media, or work-related notifications outside of work hours.

Finally, it's important to remember that balance is not a destination, but rather a journey. There will be times when work demands more of your time and attention, and other times when personal life takes priority. The key is to be flexible and adaptable, and to make adjustments as needed to ensure that you are living a balanced and fulfilling life.

In conclusion, balancing work and life is a critical aspect of high performance. By understanding what is truly important to you, setting clear boundaries, practicing self-care, being mindful of technology use, and being flexible and adaptable, you can achieve a healthy balance between work and life and live a more fulfilling and productive life.

CHAPTER VIII

Conclusion

The conclusion of this book brings together all the topics and subtopics covered in the previous chapters to provide a comprehensive overview of the productivity paradox and the various ways to overcome procrastination and increase productivity. The book has explored the concept of productivity, its prevalence and the common reasons for its decline. The psychological factors, such as negative impact, have been discussed in detail, as well as the importance of overcoming procrastination in order to increase productivity.

The book has also explored the science of high performance and the ways to maximize physical and mental performance. Eating for success, practicing mindfulness and meditation, and the power of positive thinking have all been highlighted as important components of high performance. Additionally, the book has discussed the importance of sleep and rest, and the impact of technology on productivity.

The chapter on the productivity paradox has delved into the roots of the paradox and the balancing act between finding the right amount of productivity and relaxation. The impact of the modern workplace and the role of time management have also been discussed. The chapter on overcoming procrastination has provided in-depth insights into understanding the causes and triggers of procrastination, as well as the various strategies to overcome it. Developing self-awareness, setting clear goals, implementing effective time management strategies, and adopting positive thinking and a growth mindset have all been discussed as important steps in overcoming procrastination. Building self-discipline and avoiding distractions, staying motivated, and balancing work and life have also been explored as ways to increase productivity.

In conclusion, the book has provided a comprehensive overview of the productivity paradox and the various strategies to overcome procrastination and increase productivity. It highlights the importance of a holistic approach to productivity, taking into consideration all aspects of life, including physical and mental well-being, and the role of technology and the modern workplace. By implementing the strategies discussed in this book, individuals can increase their productivity, achieve their goals, and lead a more fulfilling life.

CHAPTER IX

Final Thoughts

As we have explored the various elements that contribute to personal and professional success and productivity, it is important to acknowledge the unique perspective from which this book was written. The author, an undergraduate student, has a unique perspective on life as they are just starting out on their journey and experimenting with the endless possibilities that life has to offer. Despite their youth, the author has a passion for self-improvement and a drive to understand what leads to success.

Throughout the book, we have discussed the science of high performance, the productivity paradox, overcoming procrastination, balancing work and life, and staying motivated. Each of these topics is critical to leading a fulfilling and productive life, and the author has brought them all together in a comprehensive and engaging way.

The author's approach to these topics is fresh and innovative, offering a new take on traditional wisdom. Their desire to understand and apply the latest research in these areas has resulted in a unique and compelling exploration of the science of success. The author's commitment to continuous learning and experimentation has helped them develop a unique perspective on the challenges and opportunities we face as we strive for personal and professional success.

As we close this book, it is important to remember that success is a journey, not a destination. The author's passion for this subject and their drive to experiment and learn more is an inspiration to us all. Whether you are an experienced professional or just starting out on your journey, this book has something to offer. By following the insights and guidance provided here, you too can make the most of your time, achieve your goals, and lead a fulfilling life.

In conclusion, this book provides a fresh and innovative perspective on the science of success, as seen through the eyes of an undergraduate student. The author's passion and drive to understand the latest research in these areas has resulted in a unique and compelling exploration of the topics of productivity, success, and personal growth. We hope that you have found this book as valuable and inspiring as we have and that you will continue to experiment and learn in your own journey towards success.

• • •

CHAPTER X

What Do You Think?

1. How has your understanding of productivity and the concept of a productivity paradox changed after reading the book?
2. In what ways have the various strategies and techniques discussed in the book helped you overcome procrastination or improve your overall productivity and high performance?
3. How have you incorporated the ideas of balancing work and life, staying motivated, and adopting a growth mindset into your daily routine? Have these changes positively impacted your life and if so, in what ways?

In case You Plan to answer these questions, Do Send me the answers at

theproductivityparadox@gmail.com

I will love to hear what is your point of view.

Regards
Prince Gupta
(Author)

• • •

Printed by Libri Plureos GmbH in Hamburg,
Germany